AMAZING AGENTS OF GOD

OUTSTANDING OPERATIONS

D1642541

OUTSTANDING OPERATIONS

ANDY ROBB

CWR

Published 2019 by CWR, Waverley Abbey House, Waverley Lane,
Farnham, Surrey GU9 8EP, UK. CWR is a Registered Charity –
Number 294387 and a Limited Company registered in England –
Registration Number 1990308.
For a list of National Distributors, visit cwr.org.uk/distributors
All Scripture verses are taken from the Good News Bible 2004
published by The Bible Societies/Collins © American Bible Society.
All rights reserved.
Concept development, editing, design and production by CWR.
Printed in the UK by Linney
ISBN: 978-1-78259-939-5

Contents

The Boss (or God)

When it comes to learning about the amazing agents of God, there are a few things that you need to know.

Headquarters

First off, it's a pretty good idea to know who God (the Boss) is and where He lives. That's not so you can send Him a birthday card (God doesn't have birthdays anyway) or pop in for a chat. The place where God lives is called heaven (and before you start searching, it's not on Google Maps).

God's Personal Profile

Another question you might have about God is: What kind of boss is He? Is He an evil tyrant or a kind leader?

Fortunately for us, we don't have to make wild guesses.

The Bible (or *The God Files* as agents of God prefer to call it) has loads of handy info on this particular subject.

Here's a few things that *The God Files* tell us about God:

He's good.
He's loving.
He's fair.
He's patient.
He's trustworthy.
He's generous.
He's unchanging.

He's holy.
He's merciful.
He's creative.
He's challenging.
He's exciting.
He's surprising.

These are just some aspects of God's personality profile, but they should be enough to convince an agent that God is someone who's well worth getting to know and accepting a mission from!

God's backstory

All amazing agents are aware that their boss, God, actually created everything – and by that I mean the sun and moon, stars and Mars, dogs and frogs, pears and bears, ants and pants (sorry, I got carried away with my rhyming – God didn't make that last thing!) – and, of course, let's not forget He made you and me!

In fact, God made the whole kit and caboodle (everything)!

To round things off, God gave us humans the important mission of looking after planet Earth. And why did He do that? Because people are the pinnacle of His creation and as far as God is concerned, we're the bee's knees. He's mad about us (not mad *at* us!). That's why God made human beings in the first place – so that we could be His friends and could go on exciting missions with Him.

Sad to say, things didn't quite go to plan and the world's very first people (Adam and Eve) found themselves doing something God had given instructions not to do.

And this neatly leads us on to some other important information all agents of God need to know.

God's nemesis

God has an arch enemy.

It's hard to believe when you know how good God is, but it's the truth.

The God Files call God's number one enemy 'Satan' (also known as the devil). It was Satan who was responsible for persuading Adam and Eve to reject God's mission for them and to disobey Him.

Not only did this ruin Adam and Eve's friendship with God, but it gave Satan the chance to let loose all of the bad things that now spoil our world.

However, God had a plan – which makes now a good time to introduce you to Jesus.

God's right-hand man

Jesus is God's Son, His main man on all secret missions. If you've ever seen a Christmas nativity play then you'll know a thing or two about Him. Jesus came to earth undercover, as a baby. No one was expecting that.

Jesus didn't start life as a baby in a manger. Before that amazing event, He lived in heaven – but God had a special mission for Him. Around two thousand years ago, crazy as it sounds, He was born into a human body. There's no point in trying to work out how it happened. If God has the power to create the whole universe, anything is possible!

The point of the mission wasn't for Jesus to bring back intelligence to God about what it felt like to be a human being (as interesting as this might have been). No, the primary mission was to repair the broken relationship human beings had with God.

The secondary mission was to get rid of all the grot that arch enemy Satan had brought into the world. You can find out exactly how Jesus got on with His mission at the end of this book.

How to use *The God Files*

As an agent progresses in their training, they will have access to more knowledge about God through *The God Files*.

If you've never got around to taking a look inside *The God Files* (and even if you have), you might be wondering where on earth to begin.

So let me help you out. For starters, *The God Files* isn't just one big book, but 66 smaller books all rolled into one.

And all of these books have names, such as Genesis (which is right at the very beginning) and Revelation (which is at the very end). Some of the books have more than one section (like a sort of part one and part two).

Most books in *The God Files* have chapters like normal books, and verses like those in poems.

So, supposing you wanted to check out chapter 13 and verse 35 of *The God Files* book John, here's how you'll usually find it written: **John 13:35.**

It's a message every agent of God needs to know, so why not go ahead and look it up?

Oh yes, there's just one more thing – *The God Files* is not only divided into books but it's also in two sections. The Old Testament (all the stuff that happened before Jesus was born) and the New Testament (all the stuff that happened around the time of Jesus' birth and onwards).

God is recruiting more agents!

Also, at the end of this book, you'll find out how to become an agent of God yourself – should you choose to accept the mission. No skipping the pages, though! Let's find out first, from the reports of previous agents, what could be involved in working for God.

This book features six amazing agents of God, and the adventures they had while carrying out their assignments from Him. You can read their full report in *The God Files,* but this book picks out some of the highlights of their exciting missions to give you a taste of what being an agent of God is all about.

Look out for the following symbols:

 Inside Information so that you can learn a thing or two and become an amazing agent of God as well.

 Fascinating Facts to give you the low down on things you maybe didn't know but which I'm sure you'll find interesting.

 Licensed to Laugh is your official permission to have a good old chuckle.

Finally, when it comes to being an agent of God, as well as knowing who God is, it's good to explain what an agent actually does. So, just in case you didn't know: an agent is someone who acts on behalf of someone else as their representative. The agents we are going to read about were acting on behalf of God, with His authority and with His power.

Wow – what an awesome privilege and incredible responsibility!

Right, time to read the file on our first agent of God.

AGENT JOHN THE BAPTIST

Agent Profile

CODENAME: John the Baptist.

ACTIVE: AD 30? (Scroll down to the Fascinating Fact feature to discover why there's a question mark about this date.)

OPERATIONAL BASE: Israel (in particular, the wilderness bits).

CLAIMS TO FAME: Was filled with the Holy Spirit before he was born and got to baptise none other than Jesus himself!

The year of Jesus' birth is used as the basis for counting years. The time before Jesus was born is traditionally referred to as BC (Before Christ) and the time after his birth as AD (*Anno Domini*, which is Latin for 'the year of the Lord'). Unfortunately, it would appear that the people who worked out these dates were probably a few years amiss and it's now generally thought that Jesus was born sometime between 4 BC and 6 BC.

Obviously, Jesus couldn't *actually* be born a few years before his own birth (that would be impossible!) but as far as the calendars go that's the way it looks. Which is why I've put a question mark beside the active date of John the Baptist. We traditionally date the time John entered active service as an agent of God at around the same time Jesus did, which is AD 30. So, in this book we'll be sticking with that dating system even if it isn't completely accurate. Hope that all makes sense.

FF

Agent's background file

John's dad, Zechariah, was a priest at the Temple in Jerusalem. According to *The God Files*, Zechariah and his wife Elizabeth were getting on a bit (sorry to be so blunt about it) and weren't able to have kids. One day, while Zechariah was on duty in the Temple, he had the surprise of his life. An angel suddenly appeared and announced that he had a rather important message from God. Zechariah was scared witless so the angel quickly sought to calm his fears.

'Don't be afraid, Zechariah! God has heard your prayer, and your wife Elizabeth will bear you a son. You are to name him John.'

Wow! Wait until he told Elizabeth. But not so fast. The angel hadn't quite finished.

'[John] will be a great man in the Lord's sight. He must not drink any wine or strong drink. From his very birth he will be filled with the Holy Spirit, and he will bring back many of the people of Israel to the Lord their God.'

This was a long message. I'll bet Zechariah wished he'd taken notes. The angel continued.

'He will go ahead of the Lord, strong and mighty like the prophet Elijah. He will bring fathers and children together again; he will turn disobedient people back to the way of thinking of the righteous; he will get the Lord's people ready for him.'

OK, so that all sounded wonderful but Zechariah had a question.

'How shall I know if this is so? I am an old man, and my wife is old also.'

Between you and me, it wasn't a wise move to doubt this message from God, which is why the angel had one more thing to say to Zechariah before he went on his way.

'Because you have not believed, you will be unable to speak; you will remain silent until the day my promise to you comes true' (Luke 1:13–20).

So, why did the angel put Zechariah on mute until John was born? In *The God Files* book of Proverbs, chapter 18 and verse 21 it says this: 'What you say can preserve life or destroy it; so you must accept the consequences of your words.'

Words are powerful and no way did God want Zechariah going around contradicting His message about John's birth. As you read on, you're going to find out how important John would be in getting the world ready for Jesus, and why it was absolutely vital that Zechariah (or anyone else for that matter) didn't doubt what was going to happen.

Before we find out if zipped-lipped Zechariah got his voice back, it's time to check out our first agent report, which actually happened before Agent John was even born. How's that for starting early!

Agent Report #1 –
ANGEL VISITATIONS, A MAN ON MUTE AND A BOUNCING BABY

LOCATION:
Judea (in Israel).

BACKGROUND INFO:
The same angel (his name was Gabriel) who

had appeared to Zechariah also showed up to a young woman called Mary (you can read all about her in *Amazing Agents: Megatastic Missions*) to tell her that she was going to have a baby as well. His name would be called Jesus, and He would be the Son of God. Elizabeth was actually a relative of Mary (small world, eh?), so when the angel told Mary that Elizabeth was also pregnant, she grabbed her things and hot-footed it to Judea to share her exciting news.

HERE'S WHAT HAPPENED:
The God Files inform us that Zechariah lived in the hill country of Judea, which was about 80 miles away as the crow flies but a lot longer travelling over the winding hill roads. That's quite some trek for anyone, let alone a pregnant woman such as Mary, but it was well worth the trip.

As soon as Elizabeth heard Mary's voice announcing her arrival, something astounding happened. The baby in her tummy (or womb, if you want to be technical) leapt for joy!

Although Agent John was still inside his mum, he was tuned in to the fact that God's one and only Son, Jesus, was in the room.

Years later, when John was a grown man, he would be one of the first people to identify Jesus for who He was. 'There is the Lamb of God, who takes away the sin of the world' (John 1:29), was how he put it. To think that Agent John knew this truth even as an unborn baby – that's amazing!

FF

While Mary and Elizabeth were having a special bonding time together (as well as their unborn babies, Jesus and John), something else happened to make the day even more special. Elizabeth was filled with the Holy Spirit, and Mary sang a beautiful song of praise: 'He has kept the promise he made to our ancestors, and has come to the help of his servant Israel' (Luke 1:54).

OK, so it would be a few more years before Agent John would see active service, but it seems like this was the day when God arranged to get him ready by giving him the power he would need.

If you're wondering what happened to zipped-lipped Zechariah, fear not!

It was traditional, in those days, to name the eldest son after the father. However, when the time came for their newborn baby to be named, Zechariah surprised everyone by writing down, 'His name is John' (Luke 1:63), just like the angel had said. At that very moment, Zechariah found that he was able to speak again, and he did what anyone else would do after having witnessed the amazing events of the past few months – he praised God.

Agent Report #2 –
DESERT DUNKING AND SOME STRAIGHT TALKING

LOCATION:
The Judean desert.

BACKGROUND INFO:
Having stayed in the shadows for the past 30 or so years, it was time for Agent John to be fully activated as an agent of God. *The God Files* don't give us any downloads as to what John was doing all that time, but we can be certain that his mum and dad reminded him of the special assignment God had for his life.

HERE'S WHAT HAPPENED:
John headed out to the wild wastelands of the Judean desert and began to preach. OK, so the middle of nowhere seems like an odd place to set up shop as a preacher, but apparently it wasn't long before Agent John began attracting a crowd. People flocked in from all over the region to hear what he had to say. Here's a flavour from *The God Files* book of Matthew, chapter 3 and verse 2: 'Turn away from your

sins... because the Kingdom of heaven is near!'
  Well, he certainly didn't mince his words! With
a message like that you'd wonder why anyone
would want to listen, but listen they did. Agent
John's message about turning back to God had
obviously struck a chord in their hearts and people
openly 'fessed up about sinning against God.

The word 'sin' crops up quite a lot in *The God
Files* so it's a good idea if you know what it
means. Basically, sin is the bad stuff we do that
makes God sad and that separates us from Him.

Sin wasn't part of God's plan for us but when the world's very first people (Adam and Eve) disobeyed God, it spoiled their relationship with Him and opened the door for sin to come into the world. The good news is that Jesus came to earth to get rid of our sin so that we can be friends with God again. You can find out how to do that at the end of this book on the 'How to become an agent of God' page.

Agent John used a symbolic way of helping the Jewish people to fully accept that their sins had been forgiven by God, and to help them live God's way from then on. He dunked them under the water in the nearby River Jordan and then quickly pulled them back up again to show that their sins had been washed away, and God was giving them the chance of a new start with Him. *The God Files* call this 'John's baptism' because in time God would introduce another baptism, which would be a sign that people's sins had been washed away permanently. But for now, Agent John's riverside repentance was God's way of preparing people for this.

Q: What do you call someone who likes baptising people?
A: Duncan.

Way back in the Old Testament part of *The God Files* there was an agent of God called Elijah (you can read about this amazing prophet of God later in this book). He gave a massive heads-up that one day someone just like Agent John would get the Jewish people ready for the arrival of Jesus. This is what Elijah said: 'A voice cries out, "Prepare in the wilderness a road for the LORD! Clear the way in the desert for our God!"' (Isaiah 40:3). Sounds like our main man, Agent John, if you ask me.

But not everyone was happy to see the guy Elijah had prophesied about. Many of Israel's religious leaders weren't keen to have Agent John operating on their patch, and they most definitely weren't prepared to put out the welcome mat for Jesus. They enjoyed ruling the roost and lording it over people even though they should have been helping people to know God. As if that weren't bad enough, many of them had made following God simply all about keeping rules and regulations. They'd made life so difficult for the ordinary folk in Israel that worshipping God was just one big guilt trip.

Agent John had something to say about this when a bunch of these religious leaders rocked up to see what he was up to out in the desert. These are just some of the highlights of what John said to them:

'You snakes!... Who told you that you could escape from the punishment God is about to send?'

'Do those things that will show that you have turned from your sins.'

'And don't start saying among yourselves that Abraham is your ancestor [so you don't need to get right with God].'

'every tree that does not bear good fruit will be cut down and thrown in the fire' (Luke 3:7–9).

The bottom line is that Agent John was telling these religious leaders to change their ways or they'd be in big trouble.

Agent John was a bit on the wild side when it came to fashion and, for that matter, his diet. *The God Files* reveal that his clothes were made of camel's hair (itchy, or what!), he had a leather belt around his waist and ate locusts and wild honey. Yummy!

FF

Agent Report #3 –
DIVINE DUNKING DAY

LOCATION:
The same as before, the Judean desert.

BACKGROUND INFO:
Agent John was well aware that his one and only assignment from God was to get the Jewish people ready for Jesus. Although people flocked to the desert to hear what he had to say, John wasn't the least bit interested in taking the limelight. How about I let John tell you in his own words how he saw things: 'I baptize you with water, but someone is coming who is much greater than I am. I am not good enough even to untie his sandals. He will baptize you with the Holy Spirit' (Luke 3:16).

HERE'S WHAT HAPPENED:

The God Files don't tell us how long Agent John was baptising people in the River Jordan, how many people he dunked or, for that matter, whether he was wondering how long this particular job would last. Who knows? But one extremely memorable day stood out for Agent John when none other than Jesus Himself showed up in the desert.

Agent John was rather surprised when Jesus asked John to baptise Him, just like he'd done for everyone else. *Hang on a minute*, thought John. *Jesus is God's Son. He has no sin to repent of. Why does He need to be baptised?* Added to which John figured it ought to be Jesus baptising him, not the other way around! But Jesus had His own good reasons for being baptised and He wouldn't take no for an answer.

It was what God wanted, and what was good enough for God was good enough for Agent John.

Towards the end of Jesus' mission on earth, He made it clear that every agent of God needed to be baptised as a sign that they believed He was the Son of God, and that they'd made Him No.1 in their lives. Jesus had set the example for us all to follow.

Agent Report #4 –
HORRID HEROD AND A HORRID END

LOCATION:
Prison.

BACKGROUND INFO:
Having baptised Jesus, Agent John remained where he was – preaching in the desert and doing his dunking in the river. You've probably realised that John wasn't afraid to speak his mind and his outspokenness was about to get him into big, big trouble.

HERE'S WHAT HAPPENED:
The governor of the region was a guy called Herod. He was a nasty piece of work and

had added to his wickedness by marrying his brother's wife, Herodias (in other words, he married his sister-in-law).

It wasn't just the hypocritical religious leaders who Agent John was prepared to reprimand. He also had no qualms about telling Herod that marrying Herodias was bang out of order.

Herod wasn't having an upstart like John pointing out the error of his ways, so he had the courageous agent of God flung into prison to silence him. Boo, hiss! *The God Files* inform us that Herod actually wanted to kill Agent John but settled for locking him up.

He was well aware that many people recognised that John the Baptist was a prophet from God and horrid Herod didn't want to get on the wrong side of them. But, like it or not, things were about to be taken out of his hands.

It was Herod's birthday party, and he'd invited all the top government officials, the military chiefs, and the leading citizens of Galilee. Anybody who was anybody was there.

The entertainment was laid on by Herodias' daughter who danced for Herod and his guests. *The God Files* don't tell us her name but in Jewish tradition she is known as Salome. Herod was well impressed with the girl's cool dance moves and let his gushing enthusiasm get the better of him. In the heat of the moment, he made Herodias' daughter a wild promise. 'What would you like to have? I will give you anything you want... I swear that I will give you anything you ask for, even as much as half my kingdom!' (Mark 6:22–23).

Not a bad fee for doing a short dance if you ask me.

She had a chat with her mum, and asked what Herodias thought. Herodias didn't need asking twice. She knew exactly what she wanted from Herod and that was the head of Agent John. She'd had enough of his meddling in her marriage to Herod and this would shut him up once and for all. Herod wasn't quite so keen on the idea, but because his rash promise had been made in front of all his guests, his hands were tied.

Sorry to give you the gory details but the dirty deed was done and John's head was delivered to the daughter on a plate. Agent John's body was taken away and buried by some of Jesus' disciples. John's death hit Jesus hard and He went away to spend some time on His own to grieve for His childhood friend.

Agent Debriefing

Agent John may have had his life cut short by Herod but he definitely finished his assignment from God. John was like a bridge from the Old Testament part of *The God Files* to the New Testament part. His role was to get the Jewish people ready for Jesus, which he most certainly did, just like that angel had told his dad he would, all those years before.

You can read more about Agent John in *The God Files* books of Matthew, Mark, Luke and John.

AGENTS PUAH AND SHIPHRAH

Agents' Profile

CODENAMES: Puah and Shiphrah (pronounced Poo-ah and Shif-rah).

ACTIVE: From 1526 BC or thereabouts.

OPERATIONAL BASE: Egypt.

CLAIMS TO FAME: They were a couple of Israelite midwives who outsmarted Egypt's Pharaoh, big time.

Agent Report #1 –

TWO WISE WOMEN ARE TOO WISE FOR PHARAOH

LOCATION:
Pharaoh's palace and Goshen (which were both in Egypt).

BACKGROUND INFO:
Long story short, the Israelites had made Egypt their home thanks to one of their people becoming second-in-command to Pharaoh, the king of Egypt. If you've read *Amazing Agents of God: Megatastic Missions*, you'll know all about him. His name was Joseph (Agent Joseph to you and me) but after he died and another

Pharaoh came to the throne, the Egyptians decided that having so many Israelites in their land wasn't such a good idea after all. Between ourselves, they were getting a bit jittery that the Israelites might become so numerous, they'd join forces with Egypt's enemies and overrun them. Something had to be done, and fast!

HERE'S WHAT HAPPENED:

The first thing they did was to make the Israelites their slaves. The Egyptians forced the Israelites to work on their latest building projects and in their fields. In fact, anywhere they needed a free workforce, the Israelites were drafted in. Work them hard, and wear them down was the strategy. That ought to keep them in check, or so they thought.

But *The God Files* inform us that the more the Egyptians oppressed the Israelites, the more they increased in number and the more land within Egypt they inhabited. Because of this, the Egyptians came to fear the Israelites even more. Plan A didn't seem to be working like they'd hoped, so it was time for Plan B.

This is where we meet Agent Puah and Agent Shiphrah. Pharaoh summoned this feisty duo to his palace and gave these midwives orders to kill every Israelite baby boy at birth – girls would be allowed to live.

This was his dastardly plan to reduce the Israelite population in one fell swoop.

Agents Puah and Shiphrah were having none of it. They respected God more than they feared Pharaoh, so they simply ignored his callous command and let the baby boys live. As you can imagine, Pharaoh was not a happy bunny when he found out that the women had disobeyed him.

'Why are you doing this? Why are you letting the boys live?' he demanded to know.

Their reply was very clever.

'The Hebrew women are not like Egyptian women; they give birth easily, and their

babies are born before either of us gets there'
(Exodus 1:18–19).

Who knows whether this was completely
true or not. Maybe Agents Puah and Shiphrah
deliberately delayed arriving at the births, so
that babies were already born by the time they
got there. What we do know is that the answer
they gave Pharaoh was one he didn't seem able
to argue with.

Just like Puah and Shiphrah, all agents of God
can sometimes find themselves in situations
where it is tricky to know what say. That's when
we can ask for wisdom or a download of great
ideas directly from God Himself. Did you know

that there's a whole book in *The God Files* with lots of wise sayings and good advice? The book is called Proverbs and in chapter 4 and verse 7, it says this: 'Getting wisdom is the most important thing you can do.' So, how about asking God every day for downloads of His wisdom so that you can be as smart as Agent Puah and Agent Shiprah?

Agent Debriefing

God was pleased with these amazing agents and rewarded their faithfulness to Him by giving them families of their own. How cool is that?!

Thanks to Agents Puah and Shiprah, the Israelites continued to increase in number and become even stronger.

You can read about Agent Puah and Agent Shiprah in *The God Files* book of Exodus chapter 1.

AGENT DAVID

Agent Profile

CODENAME: David.

ACTIVE: From around 1025 BC onwards.

OPERATIONAL BASE: Israel.

CLAIMS TO FAME: Killed a giant, was a prolific songwriter and the mastermind behind Israel's first ever Temple.

Agent Report #1 –
OLD KING, NEW KING, PANICKING, PICNICKING AND ATTACKING

LOCATION:
Bethlehem and the Valley of Elah.

BACKGROUND INFO:
Israel's very first king (a guy called Saul) had made a bit of a bad job of things, and God decided that it was high time he was replaced. God dispatched His prophet Samuel to carry out the task. His instructions were to head for Bethlehem (yes, the same place that features in the Christmas story) and track down a man

called Jesse. God had handpicked one of Jesse's sons to be Israel's new king.

On his arrival, Samuel quickly discovered that it was going to be a little more complicated than he'd hoped. Jesse actually had eight sons from which to choose, so one by one they were paraded in front of Samuel. However, as tall or handsome as any of them might have been, none of them were God's choice. Thankfully, there was still one other son and that was Jesse's youngest boy, Agent David. He didn't get to strut his stuff for Samuel because he was busy out in the fields taking care of his dad's flocks.

Samuel insisted that Agent David be summoned to join the selection process, and as soon as he arrived God told Samuel that he was the one. Then and there the prophet poured oil over Agent David as a sign that he was God's chosen person to be Israel's next king.

The God Files tell us that God backed up this surprise appointment by pouring His Holy Spirit on the young man.

Jesse and his seven sons may have been a bit taken aback when Agent David, the youngest, was anointed as king, but in *The God Files* book of 1 Samuel chapter 16 and verse 7 it says that although people may look at a person's outward appearance, God looks at their heart. And God knew that Agent David was a man after His own heart, unlike King Saul who seemed to be forever preoccupied with what other people thought and with trying to please them rather than pleasing Him.

HERE'S WHAT HAPPENED:

Although Samuel had lined up Israel's next king, Agent David didn't step into the job right away. Saul was still on the throne, and he was in no rush to hand over the keys to his palace any time soon. But by a strange turn of events, Agent David very quickly found himself on the king's payroll. God's Spirit was no longer on Saul and, as a result, he often felt tormented in his mind. At times like those, Saul could do with someone to play some soothing harp music. And guess who played the harp? Yep, none other than Agent David. In no time at all, Agent David was strumming his harp for the troubled king in the palace that would one day be his home. (Just don't mention that to Saul – it's a bit of a sensitive subject!)

Sometime after this, Agent David had another chance to impress King Saul. The Philistines (Israel's arch enemy) had gathered in readiness to do battle with Israel but Saul's army were in no mood to fight. They were scared stiff of the Philistines' secret weapon: a mahoosive warrior called Goliath.

Goliath was a gigantic man, standing over nine feet tall and covered from head to toe in bronze armour that weighed about 125 pounds (57 kilos). As if that wasn't enough, the iron head on his spear weighed 15 pounds not including the shaft. All in all, he was one scary dude.

Day after day for nearly six weeks Goliath taunted the Israelites with these words: 'What are you doing there, lined up for battle? I am a Philistine, you slaves of Saul! Choose one of your men to fight me. If he wins and kills me, we will be your slaves; but if I win and kill him, you will be our slaves. Here and now I challenge the Israelite army. I dare you to pick someone to fight me!' (1 Samuel 17:8–10).

You won't be surprised when I tell you that there were no takers for Goliath's challenge from the Israelite army.

Not, that is, until Agent David turned up to deliver a packed lunch for his oldest three brothers who were part of Saul's army. By this time, King Saul was getting so desperate that he decided to offer the hand of his daughter in marriage (plus some other enticing incentives) to any man who killed the Philistine giant.

When Agent David found out about this, he let it be known that he'd be up for taking on Goliath.

"'Your Majesty," David said, "I take care of my father's sheep. Whenever a lion or a bear carries off a lamb, I go after it, attack it, and rescue the lamb. And if the lion or bear turns on me, I grab it by the throat and beat it to death. I have killed lions and bears, and I will do the same to this heathen Philistine, who has defied the army of the living God. The LORD has saved me from lions and bears; he will save me from this Philistine"' (1 Samuel 17:34–37).

Although the king was doubtful as to how a young lad could do what even his trained soldiers refused to do, he had run out of options and was willing to at least let Agent David have a go. Agent David turned down the offer to wear King Saul's bulky armour, and instead chose to go into battle armed with the same tools he had used to fight off those wild animals – a sling and some stones.

When Agent David walked out onto the battlefield, Goliath thought David was having a laugh. What on earth were the Israelites thinking of, sending some kid out to fight him?

Agent David was is no joking mood. 'You are coming against me with sword, spear, and javelin, but I come against you in the name of the LORD Almighty, the God of the Israelite armies, which you have defied. This very day the LORD will put you in my power; I will defeat you and cut off your head. And I will give the bodies of the Philistine soldiers to the birds and animals to eat. Then the whole world will know that Israel has a God, and everyone here will see that the LORD does not need swords or spears to save his people. He is victorious in battle, and he will put all of you in our power' (1 Samuel 17:45–47). That was quite some speech, but was Agent David all talk and no action? We'll soon find out.

As gargantuan Goliath began striding towards Agent David, the young man reached into his bag, took out a stone and slung it at his enormous enemy. Bullseye! The stone struck Goliath slap-bang between his eyes and cracked open the Philistine's skull. Goliath fell to the ground with an almighty thud. Just to make sure his adversary was dead, Agent David rushed over, whipped Goliath's sword out of its sheath and cut off his head. Ugh!

With the fearsome Philistine dead, the Israelite army suddenly found the courage to fight their foe and pursued them until they were defeated. That day, Agent David became Israel's hero but he also became King Saul's enemy. Agent David may have brought about victory for Israel but Saul felt threatened by David's popularity. More of that in our next agent report...

If David killed lions bear-handed, how did he kill bears?

Agent Report #2 –
RAVE, DAVE AND A CAVE

LOCATION:
Gibeah, Ramah and various other places that include a cave.

BACKGROUND INFO:
Agent David had single-handedly defeated the Philistine champion, Goliath, and King Saul had brought Israel's new hero to live in his royal palace (in Gibeah), made him an officer in the

Israelite army and had topped it off by giving David his daughter Michal to be his wife.

Saul's son, Jonathan, became best buddies with Agent David, which is surprising because Jonathan would have been next in line to the throne if God hadn't stepped in and appointed David to be Israel's next king. So Jonathan had every reason to be miffed with Agent David and to keep him at arm's length. But he did the complete opposite. It's clear that Jonathan was a young man who respected God's decision over and above his own personal feelings. But as for King Saul, well, he was very quickly beginning to have second thoughts about bigging-up Agent David.

HERE'S WHAT HAPPENED:

As we've found out already, King Saul was a people-pleaser and he didn't like it one little bit that David was getting all the attention for slaying Goliath. *The God Files* also tell us that Agent David was a great success as an army officer and popular with his fellow fighting men. Saul was so furious about no longer being in the limelight that on one occasion he played darts using Agent David as the dartboard, and hurled a spear at him. Fortunately David dodged the king's dastardly dart, but this was just the beginning of King Saul's vendetta against the young man who he knew would one day wear his crown.

When news reached Jonathan's ears that his dad was on the warpath and out to kill his pal, he warned Agent David. Michal hatched a plan with her hubby and helped David escape at the dead of night by letting him down from their bedroom window. David fled for his life, and went to seek help from Samuel the prophet.

Once, while he was on the run from King Saul, David even had the chance to put an end to the king's life. He was hiding in a cave when King Saul (who was hunting high and low for David) popped into the cave to spend a penny. The guys

with Agent David tried to persuade him to kill the king while he had the chance, but David settled for snipping off a piece of the king's robe.

And even this pricked David's conscience: he just knew that he'd done the wrong thing. Saul might have been making his life a misery but he was still God's anointed king. As far as David was concerned, what he'd done was dishonouring to the king and to God.

Agent David was mortified and chased after Saul to confess his wrongdoing. Did King Saul grab David and end his life? Nope. Agent David's actions made him realise the error of his ways (well, for a bit at least) in pursuing David and he turned round and headed home.

Agent David wanted to do what was right in God's eyes and *The God Files* have a lot to say about this. They talk about 'fearing God' but it's got nothing to do with being frightened of God. To fear God means we revere (respect and honour) Him in such a way that it also affects the way we live our lives. Of course, He's still our heavenly Father but we must never forget that He's also an awesome God.

According to *The God Files* book Proverbs, chapter 1 and verse 7, fearing God is a great place to start in getting to know all about God. Here's what it says: 'To have knowledge, you must first have reverence for the LORD.'

Agent Report #3 –
A BOX BOTCH AND A BOX BACK

LOCATION:
Judah, Hebron, Jerusalem.

BACKGROUND INFO:
After the death of King Saul, Agent David emerged from his exile to claim the crown as

Israel's new king. But the commander of Saul's army (and others who had served him) were not so ready to let David anywhere near Israel's throne. They decided to pick a king of their own.

The people of Judah (in the south of the country) thought differently and were up for having Agent David as their king, so for the next seven years that's where he ruled.

HERE'S WHAT HAPPENED:

After those seven years, David was finally crowned king of all Israel at a place called Hebron. The first thing Agent David did as king was to capture the city of Jebus (from the Jebusites) and to rename it Jerusalem. He took up residence there, built a palace and as a result, it also got to be known as the City of David. (And why not?) You've probably also heard about it from the Christmas carol, 'Once in Royal David's City'. Thought so.

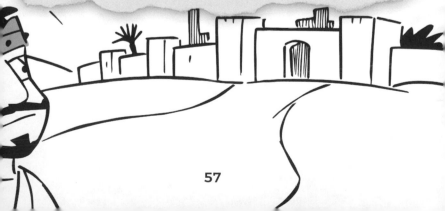

Not only did Agent David want God to be at the centre of his life, but he also wanted God to be at the heart of Israel. That meant bringing back the Ark of the Covenant to the Israelite people and housing it in a specially built tent.

The Ark of the Covenant was an ornate box that held two stone slabs (or tablets) inscribed with the Ten Commandments, a jar containing manna (the miracle food God used to feed the Israelites during their time in the desert) and a wooden walking stick that God had caused to bud. This Ark box not only contained reminders of God's power and provision but it also represented the fact that God was with them.

FF

At one point, the Ark box had been captured by the Philistine foes, but then rather swiftly returned to Israel after the Philistines found out that God was none too pleased with them for treating Him with such disrespect. The Ark box ended up being left in safe storage at the home of a guy called Abinadab. So, Agent David set off to retrieve it.

On their arrival, they loaded the Ark onto a cart and headed back for Jerusalem. So far, so good! The king and his entourage were having a right old celebration that the Ark was finally being restored to its rightful home with the Israelites. They were accompanied in their joyful singing and praising by a motley musical band consisting of harps, lyres, drums, rattles and cymbals. It must have been quite a sight – and quite a din!

But God was about to pull the plug on their praise party. *The God Files* tell us that the cart carrying the Ark suddenly lurched on some uneven ground and one of Abinadab's sons, Uzzah (who'd been helping to steer the cart) grabbed hold of the Ark to stop it from falling off. Big mistake! God instantly struck Uzzah dead for his total disrespect for Him (and the Ark).

Agent David was at a loss to know what to do. Something was obviously wrong with the way they were transporting the Ark box but, at that moment, he hadn't a clue what it was. So, there was nothing for it but to leave it at the home of a chap called Obed-Edom until David worked out what to do.

Three months later, Agent David knocked at Obed-Edom's door. It was time to get the Ark box moving again and this time he knew the correct way to do it. He'd found out that God had given specific instructions as to how the Ark was to be carried and by whom. In fact, it was the job of the Levites (an Israelite tribe) and they were to carry it on poles resting on their shoulders. But most definitely *not* on a cart.

Once again, the king and those with him made a big song and dance about bringing the Ark box back, but this time they did it God's way and this time round everyone lived to tell the tale. Phew, that's a relief.

I've already mentioned that Agent David's No.1 passion was to please God, so when he stripped to his waist to dance in front of the Ark, it was no big surprise. That said, not everyone was a fan of his dance moves. When David's wife, Michal, looked out of the window and saw her hubby prancing and dancing at the front of the Ark procession, she was not impressed. In fact, she was furious. '"The king of Israel made a big name for himself today!" she said. "He exposed himself like a fool in the sight of the servant women of his officials!"' (2 Samuel 6:20).

Did Agent David let his wife pull him down a peg or two? He didn't. Here's his reply: 'I was dancing to honour the LORD, who chose me instead of your father and his family to make me the leader of his people Israel. And I will go on dancing to honour the LORD, and will disgrace myself even more. You may think I am nothing, but those women will think highly of me!' (2 Samuel 6:21–22).

Just like Michal gave David a hard time because he put God first, sometimes people might laugh at us or have a go at us for being agents of God. Should that ever happen, Jesus gave us some really good advice: 'love your enemies and pray for those who persecute you'. You can find it in *The God Files* book Matthew, chapter 5 and verse 44.

Agent Report #4 –
A GOOD IN-TENT-ION

LOCATION:
Jerusalem.

BACKGROUND INFO:
Agent David (aka King David) had built a fantabulous palace for himself in Jerusalem, which had now become the capital city of Israel. But although he appeared to have everything, there was still one thing bugging the king. It was all very well him having a luxurious palace to live in but it didn't seem right that God's covenant box (the Ark) had to make do with residing in a tent.

HERE'S WHAT HAPPENED:

Agent David talked his concerns over with a prophet called Nathan to see what he had to say on the matter. God gave Nathan a message to pass on to David, which went like this: 'You are not the one to build a temple for me to live in... one of your sons... will be the one to build a temple for me' (2 Samuel 7:5,12–13). There was a whole heap more info in God's original download to Nathan but that's all we need to know for the purposes of this agent report.

So, for now, God's Ark remained in a special tent called the 'Tent of the LORD's presence' (2 Samuel 7:18). David had made it a place where God was worshipped day and night with teams of worshippers giving praise to Him 24/7. As for himself, Agent David liked nothing better than to spend time in God's presence, worshipping Him in this special tent.

It's clear that Agent David not only had a reputation for being a mighty warrior, but he also had a reputation for being a mighty worshipper. If you remember, it was a young David who used to play the harp to soothe King Saul. He'd obviously kept up with his harp practice over the years because if you check out Psalms in *The God Files*, you'll find page after page of songs that David wrote to God (and about God).

OK, slight problem, we don't have any tunes for them but the lyrics are still worth a read. Probably Agent David's biggest hit song was Psalm 23. Join in if you know it:

The LORD is my shepherd; I have everything I need. He lets me rest in fields of green grass and leads me to quiet pools of fresh water. He gives me new strength. He guides me in the right paths, as he has promised. Even if I go through the deepest darkness, I will not be afraid, LORD, for you are with me. Your shepherd's rod and staff protect me. You prepare a banquet for me, where all my enemies can see me; you welcome me as an honoured guest and fill my cup to the brim. *I know that your goodness and love will be with me all my life; and your house will be my home as long as I live.*

Not bad, eh? As I say, there's more where that came from in *The God Files* book of Psalms.

The subject of worship crops up quite a lot in *The God Files*, so it's worth explaining what it actually means. Worship is more than just singing songs to God, it is something that flows from our hearts. It's a way of telling God how amazing He is and how much we love Him.

Sometimes we might feel like praising God at the top of our voices and other times we might just feel like singing quiet songs of adoration to Him. There are no hard and fast rules when it comes to worship but it is something all agents of God need to make a priority, just like Agent David did.

Agent Report #5 –
A BATTLE, A BIG BOO-BOO AND A BABY BOY

LOCATION:
Israel (various places).

BACKGROUND INFO:
As king of Israel, Agent David achieved a lot of good things. He continued to lead the Israelites to victory in war against their Philistine enemies and showed kindness to King Saul's crippled son, Mephibosheth. But not everything in the garden was rosy. Agent David was about to make a mega mistake that would cost him dear.

HERE'S WHAT HAPPENED:
It was spring time and the Israelite army had gone to fight the Ammonites while David stayed home in Jerusalem. Between you and me, he should really have been leading his fighting men into war but for some reason he didn't.

Now, with far too much time on his hands, the king ended up falling in love with a married woman called Bathsheba. Her husband, Uriah,

was away fighting in David's army and the king very soon realised he'd got himself in a bit of a pickle by falling in love with her. Foolishly, he came up with a plan to ensure Uriah was killed on active service.

With Uriah out of the way, David thought his troubles would be over. But they were only just beginning. God was not at all pleased with the way Agent David had behaved regarding Uriah and Bathsheba and warned the king that there would be dire consequences for his actions. As punishment for his wrongdoing, God said that from then on there would be trouble and strife in the royal household.

Sure enough, later on, one of Agent David's sons, Absalom, went off the rails and eventually turned against his own dad. But that was just the beginning. David may have started well but, sadly, he finished badly. The good news is that God is a forgiving God and even though there are always consequences to our actions, He loves to give us second chances.

In time, David and Bathsheba had a son called Solomon, who was God's choice to succeed Agent David as Israel's next king.

Agent Debriefing

Agent David ruled as king of Israel for 40 years in total: seven in Hebron and 33 in Jerusalem. David made a lot of really good decisions during his life, which is why *The God Files* say that he was a man after God's own heart. But he slipped up towards the end when he fell in love with Bathsheba.

Agent David could have done with asking God for more wisdom. God's wisdom is something every agent of God needs to help them make good decisions and good choices. For the record, Agent David's son, Solomon, recognised that

wisdom was precisely what he needed to rule
Israel and it was the very first thing he asked
God for when he came to the throne.

Agent David's reports are helpful reminders
for us to get on our hotline to heaven and ask
God for all the wisdom we're going to need to be
amazing agents for Him.

Agent David shows up quite a lot in *The God Files*
(such as Psalms, which I've already mentioned)
but you can find the bulk of his story from
1 Samuel chapter 16 through to 1 Kings chapter 2.

Oh yes, and you can also find an interesting
bit of low-down on him in Matthew chapter 1
and verse 17 to discover whose famous ancestor
he was. Any guesses? Go check it out and see if
you're right.

AGENT MARY

Agent Profile

CODENAME: Mary (not Jesus' mum – this is a different Mary).

ACTIVE: Circa (about) AD 33.

OPERATIONAL BASE: Bethany in Israel.

CLAIMS TO FAME: Got a big thumbs-up from Jesus not once but twice for doing the right thing. Read on to find out what that was.

There are a few Marys who crop up in *The God Files* so it can get a bit confusing. But it was a common name then (as it is now) and although we use the name Mary, in their day they went by the Hebrew version, which was Miryam. If you're a smarty pants when it comes to names in the Bible you may even remember that Moses' sister was called Miryam (or Miriam).

Agent Report #1 –

MELLOW MARY AND MAXED-OUT MARTHA

LOCATION:
Mary's home in Bethany.

BACKGROUND INFO:

Jesus and His trusty band of disciples were to-ing and fro-ing (not quite sure if they're real words but we'll run with them anyway) across Israel teaching people about God and healing the sick. On their travels, they rocked up in the village where Agent Mary lived with her sister, Martha and her brother, Lazarus.

Aren't you just glad that Mary's brother wasn't from Nazareth? Try saying 'Lazarus from Nazareth' quickly. It's a right old tongue twister.

HERE'S WHAT HAPPENED:

As Jesus arrived in Bethany, it's Martha who actually gets the credit for inviting Him into their house. Jesus wasted no time in making Himself at home and talking about God to everyone who had gathered there. Mary grabbed herself a front row seat and lapped up everything Jesus had to say.

Having welcomed Jesus into their home, Martha busied herself with her household chores and, no doubt, making sure that her VIP visitors were fed and watered. Martha was a bit miffed that Mary wasn't lifting a finger to help her and said as much to Jesus: 'Lord, don't you care that my sister has left me to do the work all by myself? Tell her to come and help me!' Nothing like going to the top to get things done!

I'm sure that Jesus really appreciated what Martha was doing for Him, but this time around it was Agent Mary who got the credit for deciding to down tools and to sit attentively at Jesus' feet. Jesus replied to Martha: 'Martha, Martha! You are worried and troubled over so many things, but just one is needed. Mary has chosen the right thing, and it will not be taken away from her' (Luke 10:40–42).

There are times when agents of God need to be hands-on and actively engaged with doing things for God. And there are also times when our assignment is simply to take time out to spend with Jesus. Although we can find out a lot *about* Jesus from *The God Files*, we also have the Holy Spirit to help us to know Him personally – like Agent Mary did.

So, next time you're on your hotline to heaven, how about spending some of that time just hanging out with Jesus and letting Him talk to you?

Agent Report #2 –
LAZARUS DECEASED, LAZARUS RELEASED, LAZARUS PLEASED.

LOCATION:
Bethany (again).

BACKGROUND INFO:
Agent Mary's brother, Lazarus, fell ill, so Mary and her sister Martha sent an urgent message to Jesus that all was not well. Jesus wasn't a million miles away but to everyone's surprise,

He decided not to make the short trip to nearby Bethany and instead stayed where He was.

HERE'S WHAT HAPPENED:
The God Files help us understand why Jesus didn't hot-foot it to Bethany and heal His friend like He'd healed countless other people. Jesus said: 'The final result of this illness will not be the death of Lazarus; this has happened in order to bring glory to God, and it will be the means by which the Son of God will receive glory' (John 11:4). Sounds like Jesus knew what was going to happen and had a plan.

Two days later, Jesus finally rocked up in Bethany. Unfortunately, Lazarus had been dead and buried for four days. Agent Mary was weeping and said to Jesus: 'Lord... if you had been here, my brother would not have died!' (John 11:32).

Agent Mary knew full well that Jesus could heal sick people, so she had no doubt that He could have done the same for her brother. *The God Files* calls that faith, and makes it clear that all agents of God can have faith and complete trust in Jesus – just like Agent Mary did.

Wherever Jesus went, He not only had His fans but He also had His enemies. Often as not, these were religious leaders who had big doubts as to whether Jesus really was the Son of God. They were there in the crowd of mourners at Bethany, looking for another chance to criticise Jesus or seeing if He would make a mistake. They jeered: 'He gave sight to the blind man, didn't he? Could he not have kept Lazarus from dying?' (John 11:37).

Jesus was not impressed by their scornful attitude or their lack of faith. As Jewish religious leaders, they should have known better.

Ignoring all the tears and the jeers, Jesus headed towards the tomb where the body of Lazarus lay and gave instructions for the stone covering the entrance to be removed. *Er, are you sure that's a good idea, Jesus? Lazarus has been dead four days. It's going to pong something rotten!*

Jesus reminded the onlookers about what He'd said earlier about God getting the glory (or credit) for turning this tragedy around and, with the stone removed, He called out at the top of his voice for Lazarus to come out.

With his hands and feet still wrapped in burial cloths, and with a cloth around his face, Lazarus emerged from the tomb to the astonishment of the onlookers. The only one who wasn't fazed was Jesus. This is what He'd been expecting all along!

The God Files inform us that many of Agent Mary's friends became followers of Jesus that day. There was no arguing with what they'd seen. Lazarus had been dead and now he was alive! Only God could do a miracle like that.

As for the religious leaders, well, they remained as hard-hearted as ever and actually began plotting and scheming to kill both Jesus and Lazarus. Poor guy, Lazarus had only just come back to life as well. Give him a break! In case you're wondering, they didn't succeed. The biggest fear for the religious leaders was that their Roman rulers would consider Jesus a threat and use this as an excuse to destroy Israel's Temple (putting them out of a job) and their nation.

Agent Report #3 –
AN ANNOYING ANOINTING

LOCATION:
Yet again, the home of Lazarus (in Bethany).

BACKGROUND INFO:
Agent Mary and her sister Martha were thrilled to have their brother Lazarus back from the dead and in good health. Jesus obviously enjoyed their company and in this agent report we catch up with Him as He stops off in Bethany on His way to Jerusalem.

HERE'S WHAT HAPPENED:
The God Files tell us that it was six days before the Jewish Passover festival at which Jesus would complete His mission to Planet Earth. He would do that by giving His life, so that we would not be punished for our sins.

Agent Mary and her two siblings welcomed Jesus and His entourage into their home and laid on a slap-up meal for their guests. During the course of the meal, Agent Mary interrupted the proceedings by pouring a pint of really expensive perfume (made of pure nard) on Jesus' head and feet.

Agent Mary then wiped Jesus' feet with her hair. As the sweet smell of the perfume filled the whole house, one of Jesus' disciples wasn't impressed with the gesture and turned up his nose.

As far as he was concerned, Agent Mary had foolishly wasted money that could have been spent on the poor.

To put the record straight, Judas (he was the guy who eventually betrayed Jesus) wasn't trying to make the others feel guilty because he cared about the poor, but because he was in charge of the group's moneybag and was not averse to helping himself when he wanted to. In short, Judas was a thief and probably wished Agent Mary had sold the perfume and donated the proceeds to his coffers.

The God Files say that the value of the perfume Agent Mary lavished on Jesus was worth about 300 denarii (roughly £10,000 in today's money). That's a lot of money but evidently she thought it was worth every penny (or denarii).

FF

Jesus quickly came to Agent Mary's defence. 'Leave her alone! Let her keep what she has for the day of my burial. You will always have poor people with you, but you will not always have me' (John 12:7–8).

Not only was Agent Mary's unusual action a sign of her devotion to Jesus but it also had a deeper meaning. When a Jewish person died, the body was usually anointed with perfumes including nard, the perfume that Agent Mary had poured over Jesus. Maybe Mary had an inkling that Jesus was going to die soon but Jesus knew, without a shadow of a doubt, that this was a symbolic preparation for his crucifixion.

Agent Debriefing

Agent Mary's life is a brilliant example for us of what it means to really love Jesus and to put God first. She understood that although God is the awesome creator of our vast universe, He is also a God who is accessible. God doesn't keep us at arm's length but encourages us to draw near to Him, just like Agent Mary did to Jesus. Here's how *The God Files* book of James, chapter 4 and verse 8 puts it: 'Come near to God, and he will come near to you.'

You can read about Agent Mary in *The God Files* books Luke chapter 10 and John chapters 11 and 12.

AGENT ELIJAH

Agent Profile

CODENAME: Elijah (which means 'The Lord is my God').

ACTIVE: 874 BC to 853 BC or thereabouts.

OPERATIONAL BASE: Israel's northern kingdom.

CLAIMS TO FAME: Left Planet Earth without actually dying. Singlehandedly caused a nationwide drought.

Agent's Background File

Agent Elijah was a prophet of God from a place called Tishbe in Gilead. He began his assignment about 50 years or so after the reign of King Solomon, by which time the nation of Israel had already done the splits and had become Israel (the northern kingdom) and Judah (the southern kingdom).

Agent Report #1 –
A DROUGHT, BIRD FOOD AND A MIRACLE MEAL

LOCATION:
Cherith, Zarephath.

BACKGROUND INFO:

By the time Agent Elijah came on the scene, Israel had almost forgotten about God and had taken to worshipping a god called Baal. This was all down to their ruler, King Ahab, who had adopted the religion of his foreign wife, Jezebel. As you can imagine, God was not happy about this and Agent Elijah was the man He'd handpicked to let Ahab know.

HERE'S WHAT HAPPENED:

As bold as brass, Agent Elijah approached King Ahab and gave him the following piece of information: 'In the name of the LORD, the living God of Israel, whom I serve, I tell you that there will be no dew or rain for the next two or three years until I say so' (1 Kings 17:1).

God knew full well that both Ahab and Jezebel wouldn't take too kindly to this, so told Agent Elijah to go into hiding. Following God's precise directions, Agent Elijah hid beside a brook in a place called Cherith.

While Agent Elijah stayed well out of harm's way in the middle of nowhere, God had instructed some ravens to feed him – how kind and thoughtful! But the drought eventually reached Cherith and the brook dried up. Time to move on, but where? Agent Elijah awaited instructions from Agent HQ (God in heaven). He soon discovered that his next place of sanctuary required him to trek up country to Zarephath where God had already primed a widow to feed him.

When Elijah arrived, he discovered that his hostess was down to her last handful of flour and a meagre drop of oil. Was Agent Elijah concerned about the lack of food in the cupboard? He most definitely wasn't. He calmly told the widow to use what food she had to prepare a meal for him, herself and her son. Not only that but God had an important message for her: 'The bowl will not run out of flour or the jar run out of oil before the day that I, the LORD, send rain' (1 Kings 17:14). Sure enough, God was as good as His word and the oil and flour supply never ran dry until the drought ended.

Agent Elijah had to trust God 100% simply to stay alive. We may not have ravens to feed us our next meal or have to rely upon a widow's supply of flour and oil but, as agents of God, it's important to make relying upon God a top priority. However big or small the decisions we face, we can always ask for God's guidance. He loves us so much, He wants to be totally involved in *everything* we do.

Agent Report #2 –
PROPHETS, PRAYERS AND PERSECUTION

LOCATION:
Mount Carmel, Jezreel, Beersheba and Mount Sinai (in that order).

BACKGROUND INFO:
Israel was in its third year of drought. This was a direct result of Ahab their king turning his back on God. But King Ahab didn't see it that way. As far as he was concerned, Agent Elijah was the culprit. So, when this prophet of God came out of hiding to announce to the wicked king that rain was finally on its way, Agent Eljiah was probably a bit scared as to how things might go.

HERE'S WHAT HAPPENED:
As expected, King Ahab's opening line didn't bring Elijah a great deal of comfort. 'So there you are — the worst troublemaker in Israel!'

Agent Elijah quickly fired back in this war of words: 'I'm not the troublemaker... You are — you and your father. You are disobeying the LORD's commands and worshipping the idols of Baal.

Now order all the people of Israel to meet me at Mount Carmel. Bring along the 450 prophets of Baal and the 400 prophets of the goddess Asherah who are supported by Queen Jezebel' (1 Kings 18:17–19).

Elijah had thrown down the gauntlet and challenged the king to see whether God or Baal was the most powerful. The battle lines were drawn on Mount Carmel and Agent Elijah laid down the rules of engagement.

Both sides were given a bull to sacrifice to either Baal or to God. The prophets of Baal were to pray to their god to send fire from heaven to burn up the sacrifice and Elijah would pray to his God.

Baal's prophets went first. Hour after hour they frantically begged Baal to show up and burn the bull, but nothing doing. Agent Elijah was cheeky and even taunted the prophets of Baal by saying that maybe their god was sleeping or he'd popped to the toilet.

Agent Elijah finally called time on their antics, stepped centre stage and got ready to go on his hotline to heaven. But first he upped the stakes and made things even more of a challenge by dowsing his sacrifice with water and surrounding it with a water-filled trench. Agent Elijah wanted to show everyone just how powerful his God was.

Unlike the prophets of Baal, Agent Elijah didn't work himself into a sweat about asking God to scorch his sacrifice. He simply prayed to God and asked Him to show everyone assembled that He was God (and that Baal wasn't). *The God Files*

tell us that God answered Agent Elijah's prayer by sending down fire from heaven, which not only burned up the sacrifice but also dried up the water-filled trench!

The onlookers didn't need any more convincing. They fell with their faces to the floor and cried out that there was only one God – and it wasn't Baal. As for the prophets of Baal, well, Agent Elijah had them put to death for leading the Israelites astray.

Soon after, the rain began to fall and the drought was over. Time for Elijah to make tracks. *The God Files* tell us that in God's power, he ran all the way to a place called Jezreel, overtaking King Ahab's chariot along the way. Speedy, or what?!

But that wasn't quite the end of this agent

report. When Ahab's wicked wife, Jezebel, got wind of what Agent Elijah had done to her prophets, she was furious and put a price on his head, pronto. Bizarrely, having faced up to 450 prophets of Baal on his own, Agent Elijah allowed the queen's threats to spook him.

Suddenly, he'd had enough. He slumped down under a tree and told God that he was throwing in the towel. God respected Elijah's wishes and announced to His prophet that He'd lined up a guy called Elisha (I know, it does sound similar) to take over from him.

As Elijah found out to his cost, being an agent of God can sometimes be a bit tough. But giving up doesn't have to be the only option and that's something we can learn from Agent Elijah's story. When challenges come our way, we can ask God for the strength to carry on. *The God Files* book of 2 Corinthians, chapter 12 and verse 9 reminds us that in tough times God will give us the strength we need. Here's what it says: 'for my power is greatest when you are weak.'

Agent Report #3 –
A WIND, AN EARTHQUAKE, A BLAZING FIRE AND A VOICE

LOCATION:
A wilderness (one day's walk from Beersheba).

BACKGROUND INFO:
In the previous agent report, you heard how Agent Elijah had had enough of being a prophet of God because of King Ahab and Queen Jezebel constantly making his life a misery. Between handing in his notice and receiving instructions from God about finding his successor, something unusual occurred.

HERE'S WHAT HAPPENED:
As Elijah had complained to God that he was the only prophet left in Israel (actually he wasn't, there were in fact another 100 in hiding, undercover) and that his enemies were all out to kill him, God decided that He needed a one-to-one meeting with this special agent.

At a pre-arranged rendezvous point, on the top of a mountain, Agent Elijah waited for God to show up. He'd never actually seen the Boss in person, so he had no idea what to expect. Suddenly, a violent wind whooshed past Agent Elijah, blowing so strongly it split the nearby hills. But God wasn't in the wind.

Before Elijah had a chance to catch his breath, the mountain was rocked by a scary earthquake. Was this God? *The God Files* tell us it wasn't. If Agent Elijah thought that was the end of God's display of His awesome power, he needed to think again.

Next up came blazing fire from God but God wasn't actually in the fire itself. So where was God if He wasn't in the wind, He wasn't in the earthquake, and He wasn't in the fire? Agent Elijah was about to find out.

Right after the fire came a whisper. It was the voice of God but it was so soft, Elijah had to pin back his ears and pay full attention to what God was saying in order not to miss anything.

You'd have thought that all those other displays of God's power would have made Agent Elijah quake in his sandals but it was when he heard the voice of God that he covered his face with a cloak – awestruck by being in God's presence.

It was at this point that God asked Elijah what he was doing. Of course, God already knew the answer but it gave Agent Elijah the chance to tell God how he felt about things, and it gave God the chance to relieve him of his duties.

We can only speculate as to why God showed up to Agent Elijah in such a way. Maybe it was to remind Elijah that He wasn't a distant God but someone who talks to us personally, in a calm, quiet voice, making us feel like we're the most important person in the world. Even though Agent Elijah may have had enough of being a prophet, God still took time to show him that He cared about him as a human being.

Agent Report #4 –
A FALL, FIRE AND A FAREWELL

LOCATION:
Samaria.

BACKGROUND INFO:
We've fast forwarded a few years – King Ahab has died and Ahaziah (his son) has succeeded him as Israel's new king. Ahaziah was a chip off the old block and as wicked as his mum (Queen Jezebel) and his dad. On the plus side, he was only on the throne for a couple of years and then disaster struck. Intrigued? Read on...

HERE'S WHAT HAPPENED:
King Ahaziah fell from the balcony of his palace and was seriously injured. Rather than turn to Israel's God, he sent messengers to consult the god of the Philistines to find out if he'd get better. Meanwhile, an angel of God rendezvoused with Agent Elijah and dispatched him on a mission to confront Ahaziah's messengers.

Elijah intercepted them and sent them back to the king with a message of his own: 'Why are you going to consult Baalzebub, the god of Ekron? Is it because you think there is no god in Israel? Tell the king that the LORD says, "You will not recover from your injuries; you will die!"' (2 Kings 1:3–4). They turned back and headed for the palace.

When King Ahaziah heard what they had to say, he soon realised that it was none other than his parents' arch enemy, Elijah, who was now making life difficult for him as well. He had no time for this meddling prophet of God, so sent 50 of his fighting men with a commanding officer to capture Agent Elijah. God was having none of it and sent down fire from heaven to destroy Ahaziah's hit squad.

So the king sent *another* 50 of his fighting men with a commanding officer to capture Agent Elijah. Guess what? The same thing happened to them – they were burnt to a cinder. When King Ahaziah sent a *third* fighting force to apprehend Agent Elijah, the commanding officer had the good sense to beg Elijah for mercy and to spare their lives.

God's angel told Elijah that it was OK to accompany the men to the palace and not to be afraid. Credit goes to Agent Elijah because when he entered the king's room, he didn't change his tune. He repeated the message: because Ahaziah had turned his back on God (and gone after other gods instead), he would not recover.

And lo and behold, that's precisely what happened. King Ahaziah popped his clogs and his brother, Joram, succeeded him.

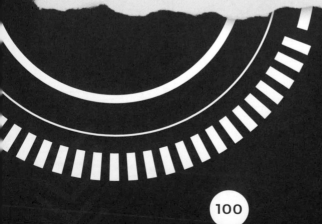

Prophets like Agent Elijah pop up all through the Old Testament part of *The God Files* and also in the New Testament part. Simply put, a prophet is someone who hears from God and then passes on that information to the people who need to hear it. Sometimes it's to give a heads-up that God is going to do something (like send Jesus to the world) and sometimes it might be a warning for people to mend their ways and start to do things God's way.

In *The God Files* it also talks about *all* agents of God being able to prophesy. So what sort of things are we supposed to hear from the Boss (God) and communicate to other people? The answer to that question is found in *The God Files* book of 1 Corinthians, chapter 14 and verse 3: 'But those who proclaim God's message speak to people and give them help, encouragement, and comfort.'

Agent Report #5 –
LOTS OF PROPHETS AND ONE BIG LOSS

LOCATION:
Gilgal, Bethel, Jericho and the River Jordan.

BACKGROUND INFO:
Agent Elijah had been given a heads-up from HQ (God in heaven) that his time on earth was up. Elisha, his successor, was also well aware of this and planned to be by his side when he departed.

HERE'S WHAT HAPPENED:
Agent Elijah was a man on a mission to be at the right place, at the right time to catch his flight to heaven. More of that soon!

Agent Elijah left Gilgal and made tracks for Bethel with Elisha following hot on his heels. On arrival in Bethel, Elisha was confronted by a bunch of local prophets who were keen to tell him what he already knew. 'Do you know that the LORD is going to take your master away from you today?' (2 Kings 2:3). I guess Elisha was too

upset at the thought of losing Elijah because *The God Files* tell us that he didn't want to talk about it.

But no time to rest. Their next stop was Jericho, and Agent Elijah couldn't persuade Elisha to stay put in Bethel. Word had obviously reached the prophets in Jericho about Agent Elijah's imminent departure because a bunch of local prophets from there were also keen to tell Elisha what he already knew. 'Do you know that the LORD is going to take your master away from you today?' And once again, Elisha blanked the conversation. He was in no mood to be reminded of the inevitable.

But no time to rest. Their next stop was the River Jordan. No prizes for guessing who should come out to meet them on their arrival. Yep, another bunch of local prophets, but if these guys knew what was going to happen to Elijah, they didn't let on. They just stood on the sidelines and watched what happened next.

Agent Elijah took off his cloak, rolled it up and struck the river with it. To everyone's amazement the waters parted and Elijah and Elisha crossed to the other side on dry land. Wow!

As a reward for his persistence, Agent Elijah kindly asked Elisha for any last requests. Elisha knew just what he wanted: 'Let me receive the share of your power that will make me your successor'. Elijah didn't know whether he would

be able to grant his request, so he replied: 'you will receive it if you see me as I am being taken away from you; if you don't see me, you won't receive it' (2 Kings 2:9–10). Elisha had stuck to him like glue up to this point so Agent Elijah wasn't going to stop him now.

As the pair of prophets were talking, a chariot appeared as if from nowhere. In fact, it had come from heaven and *The God Files* describes it as a chariot of fire pulled by blazing horses. Was this Agent Elijah's taxi sent from God to take him to heaven? Technically, it wasn't. The fiery chariot came between them and then a whirlwind scooped Agent Elijah up into heaven and out of sight for ever.

Elisha was distraught at losing his best buddy but, by way of consolation, he did get what he asked for – a double dose of the same power that had been on Agent Elijah.

Agent Elijah wasn't the only person to leave this world without actually dying first. The other was a guy called Enoch, who *The God Files* inform us walked faithfully with God and then God took him. Enoch was also dad to the world's oldest man ever – Methuselah who lived a whopping 969 years. That's an awful lot of birthday cakes!

FF

Agent Debriefing

Agent Elijah's assignment was to bring Israel back to God, and to tell its leaders that God wouldn't tolerate them worshipping any other god but Him. Even though Agent Elijah struggled under the pressure of being a prophet, he had some outstanding successes, which is why we can most definitely call him an amazing agent of God.

You can read about Agent Elijah in *The God Files* books of 1 Kings from chapter 17 through to 2 Kings chapter 2.

HOW TO BECOME AN AGENT OF GOD

Becoming an agent of God begins with deciding that you no longer want to live your life without God, and starting to believe that Jesus has made it possible for you to reconnect with Him.

If you want to do that, here's a prayer that you can pray:

Dear God,
I'm sorry for all the bad things I've done,
but thank You for sending Jesus to take the punishment for my sin so that I can be completely forgiven, and You and I can be friends again. From now on, I want You to be my God so that I can live every day with You, and for You, as an agent of God.
Please fill me with Your Holy Spirit
to help me do this.
Amen.

If you prayed that prayer, then congratulations! Now you are not only friends with God, but also an agent of God!

Why not tell a Christian you know and trust what you've just prayed? Maybe they can help you begin your new life with God by suggesting a good agent outpost (a church) where you can meet other agents of God and learn more about Him.

OVER AND OUT!

Open up *The God Files* again and comb through more reports of the amazing agents of God!

Discover why these Old and New Testament characters accepted missions that led to amazing adventures and a deeper faith in their boss (God).

Get to know the profile, background and achievement of agents Deborah, Moses, Hannah, Samuel and Philip.
ISBN: 978-1-78259-938-8

Read the agent reports of Old and New Testament characters Abram, Daniel, Ruth, Paul and Priscilla.
ISBN: 978-1-78259-827-5

This time, you'll be looking at Bible characters such as Joseph, Esther, Peter and Mary as agents on a mission from God.
ISBN: 978-1-78259-804-6

To order visit **cwr.org.uk/shop**
Also available from Christian bookshops.

Discover more stories in the Bible than ever before!

Each book retells 50 Bible stories, each with a crazy cartoon and a cliff-hanger ending.
So what are you waiting for? Get reading!

Author: Andy Robb

To order visit **cwr.org.uk/shop**
Also available from Christian bookshops.

Meet Professor Bumblebrain!

Uncover mind-boggling facts about God and His Word with brilliant and barmy Bible buff Professor Bumblebrain. With colourful cartoons and (ahem) 'hilarious' jokes, these books address some really big questions!

Author: Andy Robb

To order visit **cwr.org.uk/shop**
Also available from Christian bookshops.

Books filled with fun, facts and stories

Dive into the wonderful world of the Topz Gang, and join them on adventures to discover more about God...

Follow the hilarious adventures of Sparky Smart and her family and discover that nothing can get in the way of God's unconditional love...

Or explore 40 Old and New Testament stories of the Bible, including some of the more mysterious bits!

To order visit **cwr.org.uk/shop**
Also available from Christian bookshops.

Get to know the Bible every day!

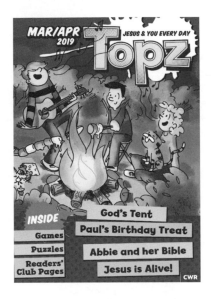

Have a great time reading the Bible every day and learning more about being God's friend. Join the Topz Gang on their adventures, with codes and puzzles to solve, and prayers and action ideas. There are competitions to enter and fun special features to enjoy!

Available as individual copies or as a one-year subscription.

To order visit **cwr.org.uk/shop**
Also available from Christian bookshops.